My Mum makes
The
BEST Cakes

Routledge
Taylor & Francis Group

LONDON AND NEW YORK

First published 2013 by Speechmark Publishing Ltd

Published 2017 by Routledge
2 Park Square, Milton Park, Abingdon, Oxon OX14 4RN
711 Third Avenue, New York, NY 10017, USA

Routledge is an imprint of the Taylor & Francis Group, an informa business

Text Copyright © Jo Johnson 2012
Illustrations Copyright © Lauren Densham 2012

British Library Cataloguing in Publication Data
A catalogue record for this book is available from the British Library

ISBN 9780863889868 (pbk)

My Mum makes

The
BEST Cakes

Routledge
Taylor & Francis Group

LONDON AND NEW YORK

NOTES FOR PARENTS

"How can we talk to our children about brain injury?" This is a regularly asked question by individuals who have suffered a brain injury and their respective partners. The answer is straightforward: you can talk to them about it in the same way that you talk to them about all other aspects of your lives as a family.

Honesty is vital; children always know if things are being kept from them and consequently imagine things to be much worse. They need to know the facts about brain injury in a way that is relevant to them. Lots of children like to know about what happened and when, if they were too young to remember. They need to know that they won't get a brain injury by just banging their head. They need reassurance that what has happened and the consequences are not their fault.

Your child needs to understand that it is not a terminal disease and they need to be given information about the most common issues after a brain injury, for example: forgetfulness, reduced tolerance to noise and temper problems.

They need an opportunity to ask questions and to feel that it is all right to ask questions at any time in the future. As they get older they will want more information as their cognitive ability improves.

This book has been designed so that children of between five and eight can read it independently. However, ideally it should be used with an adult to facilitate discussion about all aspects of family life and to enhance general emotional wellbeing. This book deliberately makes brain injury one of many things going on for this small group of children because for most children it is only one of many issues in their family life.

This story is intended to emphasise that all families are different, with their own strengths and weaknesses and different experiences. Brain injury is another experience that some people encounter and others do not.

Use the book as a template to enable you to create your own family book that is personal to your family life. Together, create a book that includes the names and adventures of your family and the positive and negative experiences that brain injury creates.

Jo Johnson

Consultant Neuropsychologist

Other books by the same author include:

My Dad makes the Best Boats

For younger children who have a Dad with a brain Injury

"My Parent has a Brain Injury" ... a guide for young people

Aimed at older children and teenagers

Leah is six today. She is very excited.

Her Mum has made her a cake that looks like a princess castle.

Holly, Alex, Isaac and Joshua come to Leah's party. They love the cake. Leah's brother Ben loves it too!

"Your Mum makes the best cakes, I wish my Mum could make such great cakes," says Holly.

How old will you be on your next birthday?

The next day Leah and Alex are playing in the garden.

Leah's Mum sits in the deck chair and watches them run about and play.

"My Mum is always too busy to watch me play, I like your Mum," Alex tells Leah.

Leah's Mum laughs. "I have to sit," she says, "I get very tired."

Does your Mum get tired?

Leah is learning to read. Every evening before she goes to bed, her Mum listens to her read. Leah's favourite books are about Biff and Chip. Her books are funny and Leah and her Mum laugh a lot.

"Let's read this book tonight," says Mum.

"Oh Mum, we looked at that book yesterday," says Leah. "You are always forgetting things."

Mum smiles. "I know, but at least I have you to remember for me."

What does your Mum forget?

Today is sports day. Leah, Alex and Holly's team win the egg and spoon race. They are very excited.

Holly's Mum runs in the Mummy's race but Leah's Mum has a bad leg so she can't run in the race. Leah and her Mum cheer for Holly's Mum and clap when she wins.

The children go back into school and the Mums and Dads go home.

What things does your Mum find difficult?

"Why can't your Mum run?" asks Holly.

"She had a car crash when I was four and hurt her head. Now she has a brain injury." Leah says.

Alex says, "I banged my head today. Do I have a brain injury?" Leah thought that was funny.

The girls laughed, "Boys are so silly!"

Leah told her friends, "You don't get a brain injury from a little bump. My Mum hurt her head very badly in a big car crash. Now she has a bad leg, she forgets things and says the wrong words. Sometimes she gets cross or sad."

Leah is eating her dinner. It's her favourite, mashed potato, sausages and carrots.

"Dad," she says, "at school I told Holly and Alex about Mum's car crash."

"That's great," Dad answers. "It is good to talk to your friends about what happened to Mum."

"I wish Mum had not had her crash," says Leah.

"So do I," says Dad and gives Leah a hug.

Is your Mum different since her brain injury?

At breakfast the next day Leah is still thinking about her Mum and the crash.

She says, "why did my Mum have to get hurt? I liked my Mum when she did not shout and get tired."

"I know," says Dad, "but now your Mum has more time to read books with you and make cakes."

Leah felt happy she and her Mum could still have nice times together.

What do you like doing with your Mum?

Holly is having tea with her Mum. She is sad. She is worried about Leah's Mum.

"Leah said her Mum's brain injury won't get better," says Holly.

"I know," says Holly's Mum. "Leah's Mum might not go back to how she was before her crash, but she can still do lots of great things with Leah and Ben."

Holly felt happy that Leah's Mum could keep making great cakes.

What makes you feel worried?

Mum is cross. Leah's brother Ben has got paint on the chair.

Mum shouts at Ben and says bad words.

Ben cries. Dad and Leah feel upset.

When Mum has gone upstairs, Leah says, "it frightens me when Mum shouts at us, I don't think she loves us anymore."

What frightens you?

"No," says Dad, "Mum shouts because of her brain injury. It is not your fault. She still loves you and Ben very much."

Mum comes downstairs and is not shouting anymore. Mum gets some chocolate cake and lemonade. They all eat it and everyone feels happy again.

What makes you happy?

Today is Mother's Day. Leah's teacher is called Miss Underwood. Leah and Holly like Miss Underwood, she is fun. The teacher gives them all a piece of paper with hearts on it.

"Write something nice about your Mum," says Miss Underwood.

Think of something you could do for your Mum on Mother's Day

Holly writes, "I love my Mum, she can run fast."

Alex writes, "my Mum reads me stories, I love stories."

Leah writes, "my Mum makes the best cakes."

They all stick their pictures on a big poster. The poster says, "we love our Mums!"

Write something nice about your Mum.

Today is Leah's birthday, she is seven. Holly, Alex, Reuben and Kaiya come to her party. Mum carries out a chocolate cake with bright pink icing and a cherry on the top.

"Wow," says Reuben, "your Mum makes the best cakes."

"I know," smiles Leah, "she is the best Mum!"

What colour was your Birthday cake?

My Mum makes

The

BEST

Cakes

Activity pages

Spot the Difference

Can you spot the 13 differences?

Wordsearch

Activity Page

T	R	M	U	R	B	E	R	E	C	C	R	H	B
R	M	R	I	A	H	C	L	E	E	H	W	S	Z
A	G	N	I	S	S	E	C	O	R	P	B	F	X
U	I	A	N	I	A	R	B	S	E	B	O	L	R
M	O	G	J	C	L	N	S	L	B	K	K	S	Y
A	I	R	U	O	Q	A	Y	L	E	I	C	L	R
B	F	O	R	G	E	T	F	U	L	T	H	S	E
I	I	T	Y	N	M	T	R	R	L	E	E	Y	G
L	A	C	E	I	O	E	G	A	U	T	C	M	R
I	B	O	X	T	T	N	M	O	M	E	L	P	U
T	I	D	I	I	I	T	H	O	U	G	H	T	S
Y	C	R	R	V	O	I	H	Q	R	K	M	O	K
H	E	D	A	E	N	O	Z	C	F	Y	N	M	J
L	M	H	A	M	S	N	E	K	O	R	T	S	D

Brain	Injury	Forgetful
Cognitive	Emotions	Organ
Thoughts	Cells	Surgery
Trauma	Symptoms	Attention
Memory	Ability	Processing
Stroke	Cerebellum	Doctor
Cerebrum	Wheelchair	Lobes

Draw a picture of your family

All about me...

My Name is

These are the people in my family

Draw your favourite food on the plate below

I don't like eating...

Colour the shape below in your favourite colour

The colour of my eyes is

Draw your house in the cloud below

All about my Mum...

Here are some facts about
my Mum...

Draw a picture of your Mum
doing her favourite thing in
the box below

Name ....

Hair colour ....

Eye colour ....

Birthday ....

Favourite animal.......................

Favourite sport.........................

She really doesn't like...

Think of something you could do
to make your Mum smile and
write it in the cloud below

Does your Mum have a
favourite thing she often
says? Write it in the speech
bubble below!

Spot the Difference
Answers

1 Extra balloon on string (left)

2 extra stripe on breadstick pot

3 extra crisp in bowl

4 extra wobble line on green jelly

5 lemonade cap colour

6 different shape on baloon string (right)

7 line on pocket of Reuben's trousers

8 extra line under table

9 Leah's hair missing colour in one bit

10 extra pepperoni on pizza

11 extra star on banner

12 extra cup in stack

13 line on Reuben's teeth

Notes